Andrew Dibben's
NORFOLK

WATERCOLOUR LANDSCAPES

With Best Wishes,

Andrew Dibben

Andrew Dibben's
NORFOLK

WATERCOLOUR LANDSCAPES

HALSGROVE

First published in 2002 by Halsgrove

British Library Cataloguing-in-Publication Data
A CIP record for this title is available from the British Library

ISBN 1 84114 217 4

HALSGROVE

Halsgrove House
Lower Moor Way
Tiverton, Devon EX16 6SS
Tel: 01884 243242
Fax: 01884 243325
email: sales@halsgrove.com
website: www.halsgrove.com

Printed and bound in Italy
by Centro Grafico Ambrosiano

Foreword

It is odd how a reputation can linger even when it is wholly wrong. Only those who do not know Norfolk think of it as flat and featureless. Rather it is a county of infinite variety and charm, characteristics which Andrew Dibben captures completely in his watercolours which are a delight to all who know and love Norfolk. To those who don't they are an encouragement to learn more.

This county of the 'North Folk', once one of the most heavily populated areas of the kingdom, offers an unfolding panorama of subtly undulating countryside, of sea and sky and space. Very little disturbs the eye by seeming out of place, yet there is diversity in full measure. Inlets and bays of a – literally – changing coastline; dunes and marshes, fields and forest, cliffs and creeks; rolling countryside enhanced by the compatibility of rural architecture. Unimpressed by the onward rush of modernity, now one of the least populous of the East Anglian counties it retains an atmosphere of peace and stillness that is difficult to find and which is precious beyond belief.

For the discerning eye it is an artist's playground and Andrew Dibben paints Norfolk in all its aspects and all its moods, generally uncluttered by the rich characters of Norfolk, but alive with the atmosphere in which they live.

The paintings in this book have a timeless quality that catches the essence of Norfolk. If its beautiful places change, as many will, then posterity will see what it has lost and will envy Andrew for having the good fortune to see, and the talent to capture in watercolour, an aspect of our heritage that is infinitely worth preserving.

Dame Norma Major, June 2002

Dedicated to the memory of my mother and father,
who would have loved so much to see this book.
Annette Dibben (1921–1976), Peter Dibben (1919–2002)

Acknowledgements

I would like to express my gratitude to the following for their invaluable help in the production of this book:

Dame Norma Major, for so generously agreeing to write her excellent Foreword.
Sadie and Simon Butler, and all at Halsgrove, for recognising the potential book around my pictures,
and for letting me produce it with no hassle whatsoever.
The several owners of pictures, who allowed me to photograph their paintings for the book.
My wife Ann, and my daughter, Amy, for proof-reading and various suggestions, and all my family for
the encouragement they have given me over the last thirteen years.
My son Olly, for computer-busting sessions.

Introduction

So let's get this straight, Mr Coward: most of Norfolk is anything but flat! Yes, I know, there are a few miles west of King's Lynn which are dead flat, and then there are the Acle marshes, and a few bits of Broadland. But Norfolk *is* big; it is England's fourth biggest county, and measures 5355 square kilometres (2068 sq miles), which is bigger than quite a few countries, (e.g. Luxembourg: 2586 sq km, Liechtenstein: 160 sq km, Andorra: 450 sq km), and most of it is delightfully undulating, while some parts are downright hilly! There was a map reproduced in the *Sunday Times* a year or two ago, which purported to show what would be left of Britain if the sea level should rise by 5 metres (an almost inconceivable scenario). Basically, there was virtually nothing left of Norfolk! Had any of these cartographers actually consulted a map of this area, let alone come here, I wondered? Had they not noticed the ridge of high ground which runs right across the northern edge of the county, much of it between 70 and 80 metres in altitude, and rising up to 102 metres? (For the record, that highest point converts to 334.6 feet, and it lies just a mile south of West Runton.)

I am biased, I know; I like Norfolk! While it may not possess stunning scenery, it does have a marvellous variety of landscapes, and a superb variety of architecture; we have much to be grateful for here. My patch, which I have been painting solidly for the last thirteen years, and on and off before that, is basically the northern half of the county. It is not that there is anything wrong with the rest, it is just that I have mainly lived and explored in this part, and haven't yet run out of subject matter.

Most of the paintings represented here have been produced over a thirteen-year period. Some of them are quite recent, others older, and one or two go back much more than the thirteen years that I have been painting full-time. They were not rapidly turned out for this book, since I tend to work rather slowly, or at least that is the impression I give, as generally, my pictures are fairly highly detailed. As a result of this, many of these pictures represent two or more weeks of concentrated effort.

Of course, there are those who will say that these are not really paintings, only illustrations. I suppose that I dislike this kind of observation, because it is usually intended as a put-down; but in the end, so what? Some critics will regard my work as mere illustrations, while others see them as art, and evoking the kind of emotions they themselves have about landscape and architecture. All I can say is that I have painted the way I have because it seemed right, and fortunately, it seems to give pleasure to many people. Due to the long period of time covered by the production of the paintings, it is apparent that there has been an evolution of style, and I have found it interesting to see this laid out in these pages. I make no claims about their artistic merit or otherwise; let others argue about that!

If I should hear people say that they dislike Norfolk, because it is too drab and featureless, something which I have heard more than once, I feel great disappointment and frustration. I feel that they just cannot have looked at it properly!

Admittedly, Norfolk is not ultra-dramatic. I have been to many other parts of Britain, and have travelled to a number of European countries, and have seen tall mountains, superb dramatic coastlines, with waves crashing on to great rocks, and tall, sheer cliffs from which the sight of a grounded ship quite takes the breath away. (I am thinking back to St Alban's Head, in the mid 1960s.) Norfolk is admittedly not like this, it is quite different; there are cliffs, but most of the coastline has a mysterious atmosphere and charm all of its own, and in parts, even an exotic beauty. The countryside inland is a delightful pastoral interaction of fields, rivers, lakes, woods, marshes, pastures, and quaint little market towns and villages. A friend of mine referred to it as 'unthreatening' and comfortable. The boating paradise of Broadland is a quite unique and beautiful environment, which has finally been granted National Park status. Scattered throughout the county, there are large relatively unpopulated areas, which, when travelling through, one would like to go on for ever, because they appear so lush and bountiful, and because, in the twenty-first century, space is becoming the ultimate luxury.

Many of the pictures selected for this book depict a variety of places in a coastal strip of Norfolk a few miles wide. This strip possesses a great richness; it is not just to do with the form of the landscape, but also the varied architecture, and how that architecture has been affected by the presence of the sea nearby.

In truth, even if Norfolk's coastline is not over-dramatic, it nevertheless has great variety. It commences in the west with salt marshes and sand-flats, and then the aptly named River Ouse, whose dark, cloying mud teems with tiny life-forms which provide the diet for countless wading birds. Sand and dunes follow, to be abruptly swept aside by the delightfully picturesque candy-striped cliffs of Hunstanton. These plunge below ground, to give way to more sand and dunes, seabird-laden marshes, and creeks. Incredibly, these marshes, which are really quite tiny on a global scale, are nevertheless considered among the most important bird-watching sites in Europe. Quality, then, not quantity, is perhaps our forté here. The drama is on a small scale too, but it still gives me pleasure to see the expression on visitors' faces, when the creeks begin to flood with a rising tide, and amazes all with the speed of the transformation!

From Weybourne, the land rises up, giving the coastal traveller some delightful vistas of the sea, and of North Norfolk's own surprising 'Twin Peaks', affectionately known locally as Beeston and Sheringham 'Bumps', together with the other various hills of the Cromer Ridge. All along the coast, the land's battle against the sea carries on, but it is probably most visible to those who regularly walk along the cliff-tops between Sheringham and Happisburgh. The speed of change here can be quite frightening, where houses teeter on the brink. Further south, sand and dunes follow again most of the way to Great Yarmouth, an historic town built on a spit of sand between the sea and the estuary of a powerful river system which drains half of East Anglia. The south bank of the river sees cliffs begin again, and continue the short distance to the Suffolk border.

These are the major changes in the shape of the land along this ninety-mile coastline. This changing shape of the land is very satisfying, and even without mentioning Broadland, offers us a remarkable variety of environments to walk and explore in this county. It also offers the resident and migrant wildlife a variety of habitats. But as we travel through Norfolk, other changes can be seen taking place simultaneously; for another wonderful feature of the county is its architecture, whether it be cottages, farm buildings, or grand houses and royal palaces. They would be delightful anyway, unspoiled as many are; but the icing on the cake is provided by the glorious variety of building materials to be found here. Thus we see buildings and walls constructed of brick, with either pantiled or thatched roofs, and timber-framed houses with brick or clay-lump infill, flints, (knapped or as found), pure white limestone, old red sandstone, and carrstone. Occasionally, in some of the north-western villages such as Holme next the Sea or Thornham, one can find a cottage or barn which has nearly all of these materials in its construction. This unusual richness is a real delight to the eye, a feast of colours and textures. The Norfolk red bricks are not just any old bricks either; for all their lack of structural qualities, they possess an almost unmatched saturation of colour, glowing with a seemingly radioactive intensity when lit by strong sunshine. The contrast is simply delicious when they are seen used for the quoins of a fine flint building.

I came to live in Norfolk when still a teenager, some thirty-three years ago. I still remember being struck by the beauty of the rural architecture, and how wonderfully it sat in the landscape. A year or two later, while a student at Norwich School of Art, I had the good fortune to go on a field-trip, which eventually ended up at Holkham. I still recall seeing red squirrels there, but one of my fondest memories, is of being chided by the tutor for spending too much time admiring the cottages, farmhouses, and barns along the way! 'You're not supposed to be looking at the houses, Andrew, you're supposed to be looking at the landscape!' But how on earth can you separate the two in this wonderful part of the country?

Formative Years

I was born in Yeovil, Somerset, in 1950, the younger of two sons to Annette and Peter Dibben. My father was a baker and confectioner in the town; my paternal grandfather had started out as a dairyman in Yeovil, and Peter was the youngest of five sons. My grandmother, the daughter of an Argyll Scot, founded the family bakery business by making cakes for my grandfather to sell from his cart. Their quality was evidently quite legendary around Yeovil, and the business prospered to the extent that, when I was a boy, my father was running two shops, together with the actual bakery. My mother, Annette, was French, and had met the young Peter in the mid 1930s when she was on a school exchange visit to the Yeovil area. During the Second World War, Dad served in the RAF, eventually becoming secretary to a high-ranking officer in Supreme Allied Headquarters. For a time in 1945 he was posted in Paris, and decided to look up the young lady he had met a few years before. The romance blossomed, and Annette and Peter were married in 1946.

My mother originally came from the small town of Montargis, about 70 miles south of Paris. Her father was a representative for a large wine-producing concern in the South of France, and reasonably affluent. As the German army approached Montargis in 1940, he put his wife and daughter in his car, and they fled southward. It soon became apparent, however, that this war would not be over within days or weeks, and so the family returned home.

Discovering that the house had been taken over by German soldiers as billets, they decided to go to Paris, in the hope that my mother, then approaching eighteen, could resume her university education. This she did, but she also spent a good deal of her spare time, unbeknown to her parents, in the Resistance movement, distributing propaganda posters and attaching explosive 'pencils' to the tracks of German armoured vehicles. She finished the war as a lieutenant in the Paris Resistance, and was decorated for her service to the country.

Both sides of the family showed artistic skills. I recall a pen and ink drawing by my paternal grandfather, probably copied from a cartoon in *Punch* or some other publication, entitled 'Le Général Sans Pareil', which depicted Napoleon, but in which every line was in fact made of the tiniest writing, and all very satirical! Dad presumably inherited drawing ability from his father, and still has an exquisitely delicate pencil drawing of the actress Constance Cummins hanging in pride of place in his bedroom.

The most talented of my ancestors, however, would seem to be my maternal (French) grandfather, Jules Poux. He was a Sunday painter who took up the pastime quite late in life, but demonstrated considerable skill in both oil and watercolour. He was quite adventurous as a young man, among the first hundred people in France to own a motor car, and a great photographer new pictures recently! For three years my brother and I in fact lived with our grandparents in France, while my mother studied for extra qualifications, and so we were constantly surrounded by Grand-père's artistic output.

I was six years old when we went to live with our grandparents in France. I do not recall this as a very happy time, though there is no question that our grandparents loved us, and had a perfectly lovely home. The problem was that my brother and I were separated from our father for most of these three years, as he was unable to find employment in France, and our mother was away for a good deal of the time too, while she studied for extra teaching qualifications. So, our elderly grandparents took care of us for much of the time. As they had lost a son from tuberculosis at the age of only eighteen, they were naturally quite paranoid about our health, and obviously we were a big responsibility for them to take on. Also, Grand-père, who was already eighty at that time, had some quite strange ideas about health, partly because he had been cursed with one leg slightly shorter than the other... (not visibly so, I hasten to add). He apparently believed that all sports were quite injurious to the health, and should be banned! As he reached the age of ninety-two, can we dispute his belief? At the time of his life when I knew him, he spent much of his time, day and night, in a bed adjacent to a large window, which had a commanding view of the garden. If he were to see us running, he would rap loudly on the window, and shout at us to stop immediately! If we showed the slightest symptom of a snuffle or even a spot, out would come thermometers, and we would be packed off to bed post-haste while the doctor was sent for!

In the Old Town, Montargis
Jules Poux (1877–1969)

too. He sold quite a few paintings, but I still managed to catalogue some 65 works in my grandmother's house after his death. I was always very interested in his painting, and whenever I visited my grandparents when I was young, the first question I would ask him would always be whether he had produced any

Grand-père had a heart of gold though; during the war, he had concealed in his home a Hungarian Jew called Szigeti, who went on to join the Maquis in southern France, and later became a doctor, the mayor of Montargis, and also an MP. I think that he was quite the most brilliant man I have ever met. Another example of my grandfather's generosity, is the time when he secretly sold his bicycle in order to buy me a camera; we were quite sad about this, because this bike wasn't just any old push-bike, but was in fact an ex-army folding model, designed to be dropped by parachute. He was unquestionably taken for a 'mug' over the sale, as the bike would have been a museum piece, and quite valuable. My only consolation about this is that photography would eventually play a very important part in my future career, and so his gesture may have been significant.

School was hard work in France, a very serious business, and wasn't made any easier by the fact that everybody knew that my grandmother was a retired teacher (and very highly respected). My mother was also a teacher, and they both knew all the teachers at our school very well! There was little opportunity for laziness in this set-up! So we were not sorry when our mother revealed to us, one early summer's day, that we would be returning to England, to live in a flat over the shop that our father had just

Dog Roses
Jules Poux (1877–1969)

acquired in Bournemouth. Of course, we also missed our father very much, and yearned for a normal family existence, with the four of us under one roof (and in the same country).

Once in Bournemouth, I went to the local primary school, while my brother started at Bournemouth School. A couple of years later, after passing the eleven-plus exam, I joined him there. My school years were notable for 'could try harder' style reports! I think that my teachers may have originated this phrase in fact. I was always noted as a dreamer, my mind a million miles from the classroom! Mediocrity through sloth and laziness would fairly describe my schooldays. I had particular trouble with maths, not helped by the fact that I had returned to the imperial system of weights, measures and money at the age of nine, and had trouble getting to terms with it. My favourite subjects were art and geography, but I was also quite good at English, and any kind of handicrafts.

I suppose that the idea of being an artist had always appealed to me, although it was not particularly encouraged when I was of school age. It was constantly stressed that few artists make a living from their work, so it was hardly a good prospect! Ships and boats were another passion of mine as a boy, and so I also thought a great deal about a career in the Royal

French Interior
(My grandparents' house in France) Pastel, 1970 (30" x 21½")

Navy. I had seen and been aboard quite a lot of ships as a result of constantly crossing the Channel to visit the grandparents, but the idea was further fuelled by the presence of a Combined Cadet Force, complete with a Royal Navy section, at our school. This gave me frequent opportunities to sample life in the navy, with holiday 'camps' at various establishments all over the country, and visits to numerous ships. I wasn't so keen on the discipline however, and by the time I was approaching sixth-form age, the idea was palling a little! It was knocked on the head finally, when I discovered that my eyesight was deemed too poor (without glasses) for the navy.

Once in the sixth-form, I opted to study art, French and geography for A-levels, but, to my great chagrin, had to substitute English for geography, because the three subjects clashed on the timetable. Art was definitely the subject which excited me the most, and I must confess that I was not too diligent with my studies in English in those last two school years. It's a shame really, because English at A-level consists mainly of literature studies, and while I cannot claim to be a voracious reader, I do love reading, and cannot find enough time now to read all the books I would like! My lack of diligence then was largely down to two factors: pique, because I couldn't study geography, and laziness! Anyway, I achieved good grades in both French and art and, after a family conference, it was decided that I should attend Bournemouth College of Art the following academic year, for a one-year Foundation Course in Art.

The whole experience of this first year at art college was a revelation! Not only were we treated as adults, but also we could spend all day drawing or painting or designing. It was heavenly! Another big plus factor was that there were lots of attractive girls there too! This was really my first experience of the opposite species, as Bournemouth School was a single-sex establishment. My first attempts at fraternisation were pretty gauche, however. Mixing with the girls from the school down the road had been actively discouraged, and even looking at them was considered a criminal activity; I remember our headmaster calling back the whole sixth-form after assembly one morning to remonstrate with us about staring at females. 'This woman-gazing will cease', he had bellowed at his cowering charges! I don't recall the effect of this edict, but I don't think it was altogether successful...

During my year at Bournemouth College of Art, I remember being particularly influenced by a remarkable drawing tutor called Sam Rabin. He was definitely one of the old school (and not a young man either) and keen on the teaching of basics. He was an excellent draughtsman, and a gifted teacher, and my drawing skills improved at a huge pace under his tutelage. Looking back, I did an enormous amount of drawing during that year, as I tended to take a sketchbook with me everywhere, and worked in it whenever I had a spare moment. I was definitely 'hooked'. But, this was strictly a one-year experience; for the following year, I had to apply for a place at one of the art schools recognised to award the Diploma in Art and Design, a qualification supposed to be roughly equivalent to a degree. After various visits and interviews, I found myself accepted for a three-year course in Fine Art Painting, at Norwich School of Art.

So, I arrived in Norwich in September 1969, and have not left it for long since then. At the time, I had been worried about whether I would miss having the sea very close by; but in the event, the many attractions offered by Norwich and Norfolk more than made up for this. The city was a delight, with its ancient street pattern and beautiful buildings. My first year at the art school was as uplifting as the previous one too. I made some very good friends, and I recall many stimulating discussions about art, and life in general, which often went on into the early hours of the morning. I got on particularly well with the chap I shared digs with, Gary, who was occasionally the butt of jokes for his very slow and deliberate way of speaking! There was no doubt, however, that his mind was lightning-fast, and razor-sharp with it, and that he was also a very good painter. I learned quite a lot just from being around him for a couple of years. Sadly, I have lost touch with nearly everyone who was in my year, but I think we may catch up with each other again, through the internet; I have recently got back in touch with school-friends I have not seen for thirty-four years! Apart from the other students, I also met a number of practising artists while at the art school, some of them part-time lecturers, others occasional visitors. Some of them are quite well-known names, such as Colin Self, Tom Phillips and Patrick Caulfield, and we even had a visit and talk from David Hockney. Among the regular lecturers at this time, we had Edward Middleditch, Ian Chance (who now runs Wingfield College, near Bungay), Stuart Hodkinson, Mary Webb and Tony Carter. The principal was the charming Robert Fox.

Someone else I met at the art school was Ann, who became my wife in 1972. She was studying Graphic Design and Illustration, on 'The Other Side of the Road', in the annexe building known as 'Gunton's', after the builders' merchants who formerly occupied it. We just hit it off immediately when we met, and felt completely at ease with each other, and so the outcome seemed almost inevitable! We have been together ever since.

My second year at art school did not go so well; I became plagued with confusion and doubts about what I was doing. I think that there is a potential problem for some in the art school set-up, in that it is a strange, rather artificial environment in which to try to work. At the age of about twenty or twenty-one, excepting the remarkably precocious, one does not have much experience of disciplining oneself to work, and little experience of life to draw upon for one's artworks. A few years before I went to art school, there was a quite different approach, with a more organised regimen of life, still-life, drawing, and painting classes, with actual tuition of techniques, and little opportunity to paint subjects of one's own choosing. By the 1970s, this had changed completely, and the atmosphere was unstructured. It seems surprising now, for example, that the technique of watercolour painting was never taught in any way at all; in reality, I am completely self-taught, and would have learned more about technique and materials by attending evening classes! In 1971, I found myself surrounded by students mostly producing gigantic abstract or semi-abstract paintings on canvas, and seemingly very sure of what they wanted to do. In retrospect, I think that many of them were not so sure of themselves, and were merely producing what seemed to be expected of them. I dabbled in various things, including a number of three-dimensional wood and glass constructions, a number of

Colonnade
24" cube of wood and glass, with stainless steel rods, 1971

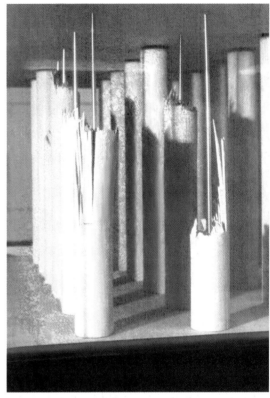

Colonnade
Detail

which I remember with some fondness; one was even exhibited in a joint-student exhibition at Norwich Castle Museum. I also took an enormous number of photographs, but only produced about one half-decent painting! I think that the lecturers began to despair of me... One or two of the tutors would sometimes tell us that the odds against any of us still painting regularly, five years after leaving college, were extremely small; they would even mockingly challenge us to a money bet, as they knew that they could not lose! Strangely, thirty years on, this prophesy is probably correct, but here I am, still painting – the one they would probably have felt most confident about betting against! My last two years at art school were not very productive or happy, but I survived, just, and scraped away with my Diploma in Art and Design.

Feeling somewhat disillusioned, I had no idea what I was going to do after leaving college, but wanted to remain in the Norwich area, and stay with Ann as much as possible. The employment situation wasn't very good in 1972, and interesting work was hard to come by. I still had my enthusiasm for boats, and thought that manual work in the boat industry might be fulfilling; so I found myself one day at an outfit called Lancer Marine, in Oulton Broad, working as a trainee glass-fibre laminator. It was a dreadful place! Half the employees there seemed to be rather unpleasant money-grabbing types, working at a shoddy full-pelt to make as much bonus as possible. There was precious little time for training, and so I picked up zilch knowledge, and got fired after six weeks! In fact, I finished work there the day before Ann and I got married! So, married life began with unemployment; an inauspicious start! I soon found another job, however, in another boat-manufacturing business, and proved my worth as a laminator there.

I had a number of manual jobs over the next three years or so. I had a very strange notion that it would be good for my soul to do quite arduous manual work. I tried working part-time, in order to be able to paint during the rest of my time, but at this point, I didn't have enough discipline to be able to force myself to paint; I was far too easily distracted. Finally, in 1975, finding manual work too demanding for my slender frame, I applied for a position as a records draughtsman with Eastern Gas, and was fortunate enough to be accepted. Life became a little easier, and I was able to do the occasional painting. In 1977, I had my first picture accepted by the Royal Institute of Painters in Watercolours for their annual exhibition. To many eyes, it was a strange subject; a picture of a boarded up fish and chip shop in the old Botolph Street. But I had found it hauntingly beautiful when I had discovered it, five years earlier; the fascinating arrangement of old floorboards nailed over the large front window, and the extraordinary glow of the colours in the tiles and bricks of the façade, catching the full midday sunlight. Another painting from this time was an acrylic on canvas, depicting the outside loo of a condemned house in Anchor Street! Once again, there was a fascination in the glowing colour of the brickwork and pantiles, and the wallpaper seen through the broken window, while the fact that these buildings were abandoned imparted a very strange, melancholic atmosphere.

During my days at Eastern Gas, restlessness set in again. I suppose that I knew, deep down, that I wasn't doing the right kind of work, but didn't have the courage of my convictions to get down to being an artist. There was still a lingering feeling that it wasn't really possible to make a living from art. I had a spell of truck-driving (delivering bread to supermarkets), and working as a carpenter. I then returned to being a draughtsman, and eventually married the draughting with the art, when I had the good fortune to be given a chance to try technical illustration. As Ann and I had a young family by this time, I needed a steady job, and this was a godsend. I took to this work like a duck to water, and was a technical illustrator for some ten years, working on contracts for companies such as Ford, the ill-fated De Lorean, and Lotus. I was offered a permanent position at Lotus Cars in 1981, and remained there until the end of 1989. By this time I had become increasingly disillusioned with my work at Lotus; the company and the industry were fascinating, but my job was becoming unbearably repetitive, and everything was drawn in black and white. How I ached to work in colour! Ann encouraged me to take the plunge, and leave the safety of my salaried job, to try to make a living from my painting. My new career as a full-time artist began on 1 December 1989.

The decision to be an artist full-time is one of the best decisions I have made in my life. Unsurprisingly, I soon discovered that it is not easy to make a living from painting. It seemed amazing that in fact I should make a financial loss for my first three years of self-employment, but that is what happened, largely due to my spending piles of money on printing greetings cards which didn't

Valori's Fish Shop (Botolph Street)
1977 (20" x 13")

sell. The sense of liberation at being my own master was quite intense, however, although this was occasionally mollified by the concern I felt at how small a contribution I was making to the family income! But Ann was always encouraging, and in the long term, I think that her faith was justified! The single-mindedness and vigour with which I have attacked my work over the last thirteen years does appear to have finally borne fruit, and it seems that my work is now moderately sought after.

I decided early on that I would like to paint pictures of maritime scenes as well as landscapes – mainly ocean liners, and this has led to some remarkable opportunities and commissions. It seems amazing now to think that I have been commissioned by some of the largest shipping companies in the world, and have paintings hanging in offices in London, Copenhagen, Oslo and the Canary Isles, among others, and aboard a number of ships travelling all over the world. But one of the nicest things to happen in the last few years followed a commission from P&O Cruises in 1993 to paint their two current cruise ships, *Canberra* and *Sea Princess*, passing each other at sea. (I had in fact suggested the idea to the company as a subject for their next Christmas card.) The following year, P&O ordered their fabulous new flagship, the *Oriana*, and Commodore Ian Gibb requested that my painting of the two ships be hung in the Captain's day cabin aboard the new ship. He was not only good enough to let me know of his choice, but also very generously invited me to come and have lunch with him aboard the ship in Southampton, so that I could see my picture in situ, and have a sightseeing tour of the art aboard the new vessel. I sat at table next to Sir Hugh Casson, the renowned architect and artist, who was the guest of honour. What a proud day this was for me, the man who, a few years earlier, had been getting up at four in the morning to deliver bread, on an exhausting 138-mile round of Norfolk and Suffolk supermarkets!

Painting ships has certainly led to some exciting opportunities. There was another occasion when I was flown to Oslo for a day, in order to photograph and sketch a liner moored in front of the Akershus Castle! Nevertheless, purely from an artistic point of view, I feel that there is a greater potential in painting landscapes. When painting a liner, everything has to be just right, the attention to detail meticulous, right down to being certain that the correct flags are flying from the masthead. If anything is wrong, you can be sure that someone will take great delight in pointing it out! I am even challenged on such details by 'enthusiasts' when I am absolutely certain that I have everything correct, and this becomes rather wearing after a time! With landscapes, people appear to be more willing to accept artistic licence, and really, from the point of view of interpretation, the sky is the limit. We have seen an immense variety of styles and movements over the last 200 years, and there is still room for more.

After art school, in effect I went back to 'basic principles', and taught myself the technique of watercolour painting. Although it is quite a convenient medium, in that it isn't messy or smelly, and it dries quickly, and so can soon be transported, it is a difficult medium to control, and unforgiving of mistakes. While most people would regard my work as 'traditional', for me, every new picture is still a challenge; I don't know how well it

Magic Moment
1993 (39½" x 24")

will turn out, and I am gradually pushing forward my own boundaries. My desire to become expert with the medium may have delayed my developing a distinctive personal approach or style, but I believe that this is beginning to come. Age does not inhibit the creative development of artists; Ann has an uncle who is a professional artist, and who decided to change his style quite radically when he was in his mid-seventies! I feel that I may be at the early stage of a slight change of direction; a couple of years ago I took myself off to Scotland in order to experience a different type of landscape, with the aim of producing some simpler, more abstracted paintings. I have been experimenting with trying to apply the same approach to my landscapes of Norfolk, and I think that this will gradually result in an exciting variation on my present 'style'.

Broadford Bay, Isle of Skye
1999 (29" x 20")

The Paintings

Great Yarmouth

Hebridean Princess *at Prior's*
1990 (15" x 11")

When I first became a professional artist, I spent quite a bit of time in Yarmouth, and produced a number of pictures, which were mostly of the quaysides and various ships moored up there. I have always been interested in ships, but I think that most people would find that there is a fascinating atmosphere in a working port, with the hint of far-off places and unknown trading links. Sadly, there is little left of the fishing industry which was once so important here, as well as just a few miles down the coast, in Lowestoft. The shipbuilding industry has also virtually gone. Apart from Richards' shipyard, there is also George Prior's repair yard; this sees small vessels come alongside for fitting out at Yarmouth, and enter their dry dock in Lowestoft. For many years they have been maintaining the *Hebridean Princess*, a small, but very luxurious cruise ship, which operates on the Scottish west coast. The ship's owners have also recently added a second vessel to their fleet.

Apart from the quaysides, there is some fine architecture in Yarmouth, and I could well spend some more time painting it; so far, I have only covered the area close to the Town Hall, but there are some gems there, as well as elsewhere in the town centre, and still a few remnants of the fascinating 'Rows' of yore.

South Quay and Hall Quay from Gorleston
1990 (14" x 11")

Hall Quay, Great Yarmouth
1990 (29" x 21")

North-East Norfolk

Happisburgh Lighthouse, Winter
2002 (24" x 11")

Lighthouses exert an enduring fascination on people, just as windmills do, but whereas Norfolk is positively swamped with the latter, we have very few lighthouses, and some of these are disused. When Trinity House decided to close Happisburgh Light, local people stepped in to keep it running, for the benefit of fishermen and all seafarers.

Overstrand
1996 (29" x 16")

This is Overstrand, and in the distance to the left can be seen Cromer Lighthouse. The landscape around here is glorious; I could have just wished that the houses in the foreground were a little more picturesque! Meanwhile, on the cliff-top, the tractors and boats await the tortuous descent to the sea down a zig-zag path. The launching of the crab-boats is not always easy in these parts.

The Fishermen's Shed, Overstrand
2000 (22" x 14")

Mundesley and Paston

Beach Boats, Mundesley
1997 (29" x 18½")

The village of Mundesley is built around a cleft in the North-East Norfolk cliffs, and has some fine examples of traditional flint cottages, as well as an excellent beach. As a result, it has become a favoured resort for those wishing to be away from the bustling summer atmosphere of Cromer and Sheringham. But Mundesley is still a working fishing village, and also has an inshore lifeboat station. The fishing boats are still in large part the sturdy, traditionally shaped beach boats, which are clinker built and double-ended, to help them ride the surf when landing. I had decided to do a major painting of the village, and felt that this view encompassed all aspects of the place, including as it does the boats and their launching tractors, as well as houses, cliffs and the sea. The Inshore Lifeboat is normally to be seen on the beach just below the little picket fence on the right of the picture. Shortly after I completed the painting, in 1997, the scene was somewhat altered by the construction of a concrete pumping station in the foreground.

Stow Mill, Paston
1997 (29" x 21")

Stow Mill stands in the parish of Paston, although it seems on first sight to be halfway between Paston and Mundesley, and I fear that I have inadvertently offended many Pastonians by referring to it as 'Stow Mill, near Mundesley'; I apologise to all concerned! The edifice has been lovingly restored, and can be seen from quite a distance to the south, when approaching from North Walsham. I climbed into a ditch in order to secure a good vantage point for this painting, with its strong foreground of wild flowers. Hay fever is a potential problem for this type of activity, as one inevitably sends clouds of pollen flying in the process! How we artists suffer...

Cromer Lighthouse and Cliffs

Cromer Lighthouse and Cliffs
1995 (29" x 16")

The cliff-top walk at Cromer, down 'Happy Valley', is a delight, and offers wonderful views of the town and coast. I have painted three versions of this view over the last twelve years, two of which are reproduced here. I am probably most satisfied with the one shown opposite, which is the most recent, and the most atmospheric.

Cromer Lighthouse and Cliffs
2002 (29" x 21")

Cromer – Seen from the Pier

Cromer
1994 (29" x 17")

Cromer has a very attractive seafront and skyline, and, if one doesn't have access to a boat, then the pier is the place to go in order to view it. Like so many seaside towns, Cromer has some delightful, exuberant Victorian architecture, as well as old fishermen's cottages, and a church of near cathedral proportions. The amazingly tall church tower served as an excellent beacon for seafarers, until the construction of the lighthouse on the cliffs to the east of the town. This view was suggested to me by some unknown admirers of my work, via a third party; I have never been able to speak to them to thank them, so I hope they will see this acknowledgement of their part.

On the Beach, Cromer
1998 (29" x 21")

Cloud Shadows – Sheringham

This is Sheringham seen from the west, more or less as it appears when one approaches along the coast road, but I have turned off down the road that leads to Upper Sheringham, just a couple of hundred yards. I love this view, with the town nestling between the 'Twin Peaks' – Beeston Regis Hill to the east, and Skelding Hill to the west. Of course, the view from the tops of the hills is wonderful, but this view is so surprising as one travels along the coast, and the road from Salthouse to this point is a real switch-back. It saddens me to think that these hills will gradually disappear as coastal erosion does its work; there are deep scars already in the cliff face, and nature generally has its way.

In the painting opposite, I have used a device which is becoming almost a trademark of mine, which is to incorporate a strong mass of weeds and wild flowers in the foreground. This particular day, the very evenly-spaced clouds were charging in from the sea in serried ranks, and casting strong shadows over land and sea in a gigantic Chinese lantern show; quite mesmerising to watch!

Cloud Shadows, Sheringham
1998 (29" x 21")

Sheringham – the Beach

Waiting on the Ramp
1999 (10" x 7")

There are many attractive rows of old fishermen's cottages near to the ramp, in what was the centre of the old village, and the cluster of buildings around the ramp itself, including the lifeboat museum, is particularly picturesque. I was quite pleased with the painting opposite, as I felt that it somehow captured the feeling of the battle against the sea that this little town and its inhabitants have been waging from time immemorial. The shingle beach comes and goes over the years, and in the early to mid 90s, I was quite shocked to see how depleted it became. Fortunately, some of the replenishment schemes appear to be working, and the beach is now usually rather wider than I have shown it here, although this was high tide.

Sheringham – the Beach
1995 (29" x 18")

On the Ramp, Sheringham

The whole area of the ramp at Sheringham is a visual delight. It was a bit worrying, around 1995, to witness the sea walls being replaced with such amazingly polished concrete; it looked rather antiseptic at first, but it does appear to be mellowing with time. The actual ramp's surface was left alone, however, and is marvellously rugged. One could think that the little boats are really nothing terribly special, most being of glass-fibre construction, but they are still picturesque, each showing some bit of custommade gear or other improvement, a quaint name, carefully and lovingly applied to the bows, and brightly coloured tarpaulins and floats. The whole scene is surrounded with the usual paraphernalia of a fishing port: nets, more floats, and great piles of plastic fish-boxes, which have mysteriously found their way from the Netherlands. Are there any left in Holland? Around mid-afternoon in summertime, the sun in the south-west causes extraordinarily long shadows to be cast by boats and gear; manna for the artist.

Blue Boy *at Sheringham*
1999 (10" x 7")

Providence II *on the Ramp*
1999 (11½" x 9½")

Sheringham Park
1997 (29" x 10½")

This is Sheringham Park, looking north-eastwards. At the top of the wood in the centre is the gazebo, and a little further to the left, and left of the bit of sea, can be seen a distant Weybourne Mill. The rolling landscape, the fine trees and shrubs combine to make a glorious spot, and the views from the gazebo are quite magnificent; however, I decided to paint this view, as the vista from the gazebo is just too panoramic to fit in even a pair of paintings – it would really take at least four!

Farmyard near Felbrigg
1997 (29" x 17½")

I spotted this scene out of the corner of my eye one day when coming back from Sheringham, through Felbrigg. I stopped to admire the scene, and just then the lady of the house emerged from behind the middle barn with a pan full of carrots and vegetable trimmings. She banged the pan with a knife and called, whereupon the sheep galloped over to see what titbits she had for them, each trying to get to her before the others! All the animals were beautifully groomed, and the chickens were some of the most handsome I have ever seen; a real throwback to former times. The former smallholding has since changed hands, and this paddock has been concealed behind a tall fence.

Weybourne

On the Shingle Bank, Weybourne
1993 (14" x 10")

The landscape around Weybourne is beautifully undulating, and the A149 coast road rises and falls with it, and offers some very fine views to the traveller. Weybourne Mill makes an important and very striking landmark when approaching the village from the east. Since I did the painting opposite, the adjoining mill-house has been remodelled, and extensively modernised, and the mill has had a new cap fitted, and all done with the utmost care. The village street is one of the best preserved along this stretch, with virtually all the old cottages being built of flints. The shingle bank here has taken a terrible battering in recent years, almost washed away at its western extremity, so that the scene above is a thing of the past. Construction of a new bank is due to begin soon, and everyone waits with bated breath to see the resulting appearance.

Weybourne Mill
1994 (22" x 10")

Overleaf: *The Coast Road at Weybourne*
1995 (29" x 11½")

© Andrew Dibben '95

Wild Flowers, Woods and Strange Little Hills

Hedgerow Wild Flowers near Cley
1998 (11½" x 9½")

One of the pleasures of being out in the countryside is the opportunity to observe the variety of wild flowers growing in verges, fields and woods wherever one goes. My knowledge of flowers was pitiful thirty years ago; it still isn't very good now, but I take a great deal more interest in the subject, and an enormous amount of pleasure from admiring them and seeking them out. I have found it interesting to observe how certain flowers are in the ascendancy in a particular year, and then all but disappear for a couple of years. Certainly, no two years are the same, and as an artist, if I notice a profusion of wild flowers somewhere, I now know that I have to act straight away if I want to produce a picture of the scene. It is no good waiting for the following year, because the same growing conditions are highly unlikely to be reproduced two years running. Apart from the climatic changes, crop-spraying has a marked effect in this intensely agricultural region. Without treatment, many of the cornfields in Norfolk would be an absolute sea of red poppies.

Roadside Daisies and Poppies
1999 (11½" x 9½")

Shaft of Sunlight, Holt Road
1998 (11½ x 9½")

Roadside Wild Flowers, Weybourne
1998 (14" x 10")

At the Edge of the Wood, Salhouse
2000 (14" x 10")

The Path at the Edge of the Wood, Salhouse
2000 (14" x 10")

Overleaf: *The Bluebell Wood, Salhouse*
2000 (22" x 10½")

Wild Flowers, Woods and Strange Little Hills

CONTINUED

Norfolk is fairly rich in wild flowers, but not quite like Cornwall, regrettably. Some of this is due to climate, and some due to agricultural practices. Nevertheless, there is much to enjoy, and sometimes, there are remarkable swathes of poppies to be found in fields and verges. In May, after the early-spring showing of primroses in Broadland and elsewhere, bluebells can be found in vast numbers in numerous woods, and soon after, campion and marguerites begin their displays, followed by the poppies. 1995 was a terrific year for mallow on the north coast, and I love to see it mixed in with the architectural stands of hogweed, such a magnificent plant. Sadly, we do not see very much in the way of wild foxgloves here, unlike in the West Country. I am told that this is due to the climatic differences. On the other hand, we are blessed with fabulous shows of one of my favourites, the rosebay willow-herb, which is sometimes also known as fireweed.

The painting shown opposite is a view to be found a little north of Glandford, in the slightly grandly named Wiveton Downs. When I discovered this spot, I was rather confused about my bearings, and found it difficult to believe that this could indeed be Wiveton Church peeping its head over the top of the hill. The top of the tower certainly looked right, with its pinnacles, but it took a deal of staring at the Ordnance Survey map to convince myself of the fact! Some might think that my depiction of Beeston Bump, with the mass of poppies in the foreground, is a bit fanciful; I can assure the reader, however, that the scene was at least as colourful as I have painted it! As I said earlier, no two years are the same, and 1999 was exceptional for poppies on Beeston Common.

Wiveton Church from Lady's Hill
2001 (21" x 14")

Overleaf: *Beeston Regis Hill*
1999 (29" x 11")

Warborough Hill, Dusk
2000 (29" x 13")

Norfolk is blessed with a number of fascinating, strange little hills near the north coast. Beeston Regis Hill, shown on the previous two pages, is a good example; another is Warborough Hill, in Kelling, with its tumulus of pines at the peak. In 2000, I found that the field surrounding it had been left fallow after a wheat crop, and had been colonised by thousands of ox-eye daisies; approaching dusk, it made quite a mysterious sight. The following year, the field was used for a crop of flax (linseed). I have painted fields of flax in flower before, but discovered that people find it difficult to understand why the sky appears to have fallen to the ground suddenly! They are indeed a strange sight, a sea of delicate pale blue flowers fading into green here and there. In this instance, I chose to paint this starker scene, as the cut flax lay drying, prior to being gathered.

Flax Harvest, Warborough Hill
2001 (29" x 17½")

High over Sheringham
1992 (25" x 15½")

Muckleburgh Hill is one of the places along the coast, from which can be enjoyed the most wonderful views, in all directions. A glance at the paintings shown on the next two pages reveals a westerly vista extending beyond Blakeney Point, and taking in the villages of Kelling and Salthouse. I only realised about three years ago that there was a footpath to the top; prior to this, I had assumed that the land belonged to the Muckleburgh collection site. Soon after this discovery, I took Ann up there: 'I'm taking you mountaineering,' I told her. She was relieved to learn that no ropes or oxygen were necessary (although the view is breathtaking), and enjoyed the scene immensely.

Beeston Hill (in the picture above), is probably better known to most people, since it is right next to the town of Sheringham, and one can make out the intrepid climbers walking up it even from one's car, when travelling along the coast road. It is fascinating what a different perspective one gets on the world from a 220-foot climb, and well worth the effort!

Near Hainford
1991 (14" x 10")

Overleaf: *Spring on Muckleburgh*
2001 (39" x 15")

Around Salthouse

Salthouse from Beach Road
1994 (25" x 16")

Salthouse is a village which seemed run-down long ago, but is now highly desirable, although parts are very vulnerable to the sea. The whole place appears to have had a makeover in recent years, and there are some fine examples of flint building throughout the village. There are quite spectacular views to be had of the village and surroundings from the heath 150 feet above, and also from the shingle bank. The latter is about to be moved much closer to the main road, so that, tragically, the marshes will become a lot smaller. Alas, the sea is too strong to resist; I have been quite shocked to see the damage to the bank resulting from storms in recent years. As with Cromer and Blakeney, the magnificent church's great tower makes a landmark which is visible for miles around, and it is fascinating to turn a corner and find it suddenly popping into view in the distance. The landscape around Salthouse is absolutely wonderful, the village being hemmed in by hills on three sides, and the freshwater marshes to the north.

Salthouse from the Heath
1999 (29" x 21")

Towards Salthouse and Weybourne
1995 (29" x 10")

I had driven past Cookies' Crab Shop (opposite) countless times, but something about the light one day caught my eye, and then I just couldn't believe that I hadn't done a painting of this subject before! Many people have since said to me that it 'just is Norfolk', and this picture does somehow seem to encapsulate the rural and coastal scene here. Suzanne and Peter, the owners, work incredibly hard, doing everything from picking samphire on the marsh, to dressing crabs, making pâtés, and serving teas and ice-creams or even entire meals from this tiny cottage.

Cookies' Crab Shop aka 'The Bait Shop'
1996 (29" x 20")

Overleaf: *Wild-Flower Field, Salthouse I*
2001 (29" x 11")

Wild-Flower Field, Salthouse II
2001 (29" x 19")

Holt

The little Georgian town of Holt has become a thriving and fashionable place in recent years, and it is certainly very attractive, and well positioned for some of the prettiest coastal villages. There are wonderful shops here, and a plethora of art galleries and antique shops. I know that there are some who feel that I have neglected the town from a painting point of view, but I have found it awkward somehow to select views which satisfy me completely; I am still working on this, however! What tends to happen with places like this, which I know very well, is that I will suddenly notice a particularly striking effect of light one day, and then feel compelled to produce a painting of it. This is what happened with the two pictures reproduced here. The little cluster of buildings at the western end of the High Street is very attractive, and really strikes the eye when arriving from the Norwich direction on a bright sunny day. The owner of the Picturecraft Gallery, Michael Hill, who is probably the fount of all knowledge to do with Holt, was eager to correct my rather vague title for this painting when he saw it; apparently it should have been 'Obelisk Plain and Blind Sam'! 'Blind Sam' refers to the rather ornate lamp standard, whose gas lantern was missing for many years, following the introduction of improved street lighting in the town. An exact replica was made as a Millennium project, using the original drawings, located in the iron foundry that had made the original monument for Queen Victoria's Jubilee! The 'obelisk' is the stone structure with the pine-cone atop, formerly one of a pair flanking the gateway to Melton Constable Hall; as a result of its move, all the mileages inscribed on the base are incorrect!

One day I was returning from Cley and arrived back in Holt in late afternoon. Approaching the High Street, The King's Head pub lay dead ahead, filling my field of view. I was immediately struck by the remarkable beauty of the shadows being cast along the façade of the building by the wrought iron brackets which support the sign, the flower baskets and coach lamps. I knew there and then that this was crying out for a really good painting, and rushed to park and make a quick sketch before the light changed. The building has a very elegant elevation even without such shadows, and the bow windows at the western end are quite unusual, their sashes being fitted with curved glass.

High Street, Holt
1997 (25" x 12")

Shadows, The King's Head, Holt
1999 (21½" x 13½")

Cley next the Sea

Cley next the Sea, Winter
1992 (25" x 19")

The windmill at Cley must be one of the most famous landmarks in East Anglia, and it has become even more well known with the BBC's hot-air balloon TV clips between programmes. The village in its entirety is ideally viewed from the flood defence bank, and is delightfully picturesque from almost any angle. A stroll along The Street reveals many fine buildings, as well as interesting shops. Beware of the cars, however! I have long thought that it would be wonderful if through-traffic could be diverted around the village, with residents and deliveries only using The Street. This could then be cobbled and paved, and would become safer and much more attractive for pedestrians. A visitors' car park could be provided on the edge of the village. A visit to Clovelly, in Devon, where such a system operates, convinced me of just how well this could work. I spent hours deliberating over the best viewpoints for these two paintings, but a good subject merits the time!

Cley next the Sea, Late Summer
1997 (29" x 21")

Blakeney

Blakeney Quay (from the west)
1992 (26" x 14")

Without a doubt, this is one of Norfolk's most attractive and intriguing villages. One's first impression of a place can be so important, and I have pleasant memories of my first arrival or two in Blakeney, at a time when there were rather less cars than there are now: the High Street becoming impossibly narrow, then a remarkably steep descent, between the prettiest cottages imaginable, their walls completely built of whole flints, with hollyhocks and valerian pushing up through every available crack between walls and roadway, and finally, the magical revelation of that beautiful view over the creek and marsh. Each time I visit, I wait with great anticipation to see how the tide is affecting the creek; it varies from a narrow trickle to a powerful river, which, of course, it is not. The water can flow at quite a clip here during spring tides; during March and October springs, the car park and even the marsh can totally disappear underwater, and waves will lap at the walls of the Blakeney Hotel. (Note the plaques on the hotel wall, showing the 1953 and 1978 flood levels.)

The village is mostly a holidaymakers' and day-trippers' mecca now, but at one time it was an important port and shipbuilding centre; it is thought that the *Mayflower* was built here.

There are many agreeable ways to pass the time; there are delightful walks in and around the village, to take in the architecture and the views, or one can simply watch the water, and the children frolicking or mud-sliding; one can get in the water or in a boat, gilly for crabs, take a seal-watching trip, or take advantage of the excellent hostelries.

Blakeney (from the east)
1996 (29" x 18")

Blakeney in Winter

Blakeney under Snow
2000 (29" x 20")

I have often thought that the North Norfolk coast has an exotic kind of beauty, particularly the part west of Sheringham. The word 'exotic' came to my mind many years ago in this context; I suppose that it is the marshes which give this feeling, because they seem so mysterious. I recently saw salt marshes described as the last remaining wilderness areas in Britain; they certainly are inaccessible at many times, and potentially dangerous. The villages adjoining the marshes acquire some of their mystery by juxtaposition, but also because of the change that has come over them. Blakeney was once an important port, and now it is alternately heaving with people in high summer, and delightfully deserted in winter – much of the time.

It is in winter that I have found it most inspiring to paint Blakeney, when there are few cars and visitors about. Late one afternoon, I arrived by the creek after the tide had filled the pot-holes. Looking back at the village, the view was enchanting, with the lights reflected in the creek, and the puddles forming a bold abstract pattern in the foreground.

After the High Tide, Blakeney
2000 (29" x 21")

Hunworth and the River Glaven

Hunworth Green and Castle Hill
2002 (22" x 14")

The River Glaven is hardly one of the great watercourses of the world, but to North Norfolk, it has a great importance in the way that it has shaped the landscape. My knowledge of geography is insufficient to tell whether this tiny river can really have shaped its own valley over the millennia, or whether it has simply done its best to find a way to meander through the little hills left by the retreating glacier, during the last Ice Age. But whatever happened, it has left us an absolutely delightful landscape to admire. The Glaven flows through some of the loveliest countryside in Norfolk, through hills and meadows, and finally through marshes, past the magnificent windmill at Cley, and on through salt marshes into Blakeney harbour. The view in the painting shown opposite is taken from a disused railway embankment, under which the river goes through one bridge, and the road to the right another. The stream on the right is in fact a parallel drainage ditch, not a strange U-turn in the river! In the distance can be seen Hunworth Church, and the roofs of the water-mill and some of the cottages.

Hunworth is a village I only discovered this year. It seems extraordinary that I had not been through the place before, but that is the nature of Norfolk; there are so many little lanes ('the tracery of Norfolk lanes', as my father-in-law once observed!), and so many places to explore. There is an interesting hill overlooking the village, marked on the map as 'Castle Hill', on the top of which can still be made out the earthwork rings of a fort, which I would guess to be from the Iron Age.

The Glaven near Hunworth
2002 (29" x 22")

Glaven Valley – West
2000 (29" x 15")

(Painted as a pair)

Glaven Valley – East
2000 (29" x 15")

Three Churches
1998 (29" x 18")

This painting shows a view from the little lane leading to Wiveton, off the Holt to Cley road. It is interesting in that it is possible to see the churches of Cley, Wiveton and Blakeney (in the far distance) from this spot. There are many places in Norfolk from which several church towers can be seen, the county having the largest concentration of medieval churches in Northern Europe.

Letheringsett from Horse Hill
2002 (21" x 14")

A little further up the valley, the Glaven flows through Letheringsett. Just below the village proper, the river has been widened into an ornamental lake in the grounds of Bayfield Hall, while upstream of Letheringsett water-mill, there is a ford, which is a favourite place for children to play in summertime. All around here, the landscape is delightfully hilly, and some wonderful views can be found. I had to walk a little way into the field to find the scene above, but part of the crop had been severely damaged by rabbits and weather; although I am dreadfully nosy, I certainly would not trample on a growing crop. I think that we should all try to leave things no worse than we found them, or better if at all possible. It may surprise some visitors that one can look down on Norfolk churches from hills in a number of places!

View over Letheringsett
2001 (29" x 21")

Wells-next-the-Sea

Wells has always held a fascination for me; it just offers so much to someone who is both an artist and a boat-lover. As with Blakeney, there is a wonderful atmosphere of mystery created by the marshes opposite. It is quite extraordinary, at spring tides around March and October, to witness the complete disappearance of the marshes underwater, and not a little worrying if there is a strong northerly wind at the time. I was sent here in my Gas Board days, in 1978, armed with a 'Gas-Tec' detector, to check whether any damage had been sustained by the main under the quay; a 250-ton coaster had been stranded on the quay overnight by high tide and wind! It took the biggest mobile crane in the country, unloaded from six lorries, to get it back in the brine.

We have enjoyed a number of stays in B&Bs here, to explore the numerous back alleys, and walk to the beach and woods. The shops are excellent too, some being remarkably quirky, and very well stocked. There is the most wonderful old-fashioned iron-mongers' shop near the bottom of Staithe Street, and a very good art gallery.

The yard depicted here makes a very difficult subject to paint in watercolour; you have to work out a strategy to paint netting, or any subject involving fine, pale lines, against a dark background. In fact, this is the classic watercolourist's dilemma. Do you resort to gouache, or do you paint all the dark holes individually? I decided on the latter course of action.

Stacked Crab-Pots, off Staithe Street
2002 (21½" x 14½")

Wells-next-the-Sea
1995 (29" x 20")

Stranded Sentinels
1999 (11½" x 9")

Ma Freen *Dried Out at Wells*
1999 (11½" x 9")

Holkham beach is undoubtedly the loveliest on the North Norfolk coast, and recently I even saw it listed as one of the top 20 in Britain in a Sunday newspaper. For those in the know, the place will for a long time be associated with the film 'Shakespeare in Love', as the final scene sees Gwyneth Paltrow walking endlessly up this very beach, seemingly unable to make it to the woods! While the acres of sand are excellent in themselves, the backdrop of dunes and pine woods (Holkham Meals), is equally attractive, and it is a rather special experience to walk through them, parallel to the sea. You can in fact walk all the way to Wells harbour from inside their cover. Only thirty years ago, red squirrels could still be found frolicking here, but sadly, I fear that they have all disappeared. At the junction of the two woods stands a very fine evergreen oak, which I keep meaning to paint; meanwhile, the fields adjoining the woods seem at times to be the world's busiest goose airport; or should that be 'gooseport'?

Holkham Woods and Beach
1995 (29" x 10½")

Salt Marshes

There seem to be rather a lot of candidates for the title of the world's, or even Britain's 'last great wilderness'! While it may seem a bit of an exaggeration to describe salt marshes in such terms, there is no doubt that marshes are strange places, and that they are not good spots in which to linger when the tide is rising; the marshes opposite the quays at Wells and Blakeney frequently disappear completely underwater. But on a fine summer's day, they can be delightful places; there is an eerie silence, only broken occasionally by the calling of seabirds, and a feeling of immense, limitless space and sky.

The painting overleaf is of the Cley marshes, which are in fact fresh water; this picture was commissioned by a gentleman who was going to live in China for a time, and is the view from his upstairs living-room. He was very particular about wanting a winter scene, with Brent geese in flight.

Blakeney Marshes and Creek
2002 (22" x 14")

Overleaf: *Cley Marshes*
2001 (29" x 11")

North-West Norfolk

Private Yard, Burnham Overy Mill
1999 (16" x 12")

As one travels west along the coast, so the landscape changes, and the building materials also. The Burnhams see the introduction of limestone (or chalk, if you prefer) to the construction of houses. A little carrstone creeps in too, and more and more of this is seen as one goes west. It almost begins to feel as though one has arrived in another part of the country, so marked is the change in character of the buildings. There are some magnificent white stone barns to be seen around Ringstead, while from Hunstanton down to King's Lynn, all is carrstone. Here and there, the odd bit of wall can be seen which contains every type of building material locally available – brick, flint, chalk and carrstone, with the odd bit of red sandstone thrown in for good measure. All quite magical! And just to add an historical footnote, the creek seen in the painting of Burnham Overy Staithe is where the young Horatio Nelson learned to sail, and nearby Burnham Thorpe is where he was born.

Burnham Overy Staithe
1997 (29" x 18")

Brancaster Staithe
1999 (29" x 18½")

Burnham Market
1999 (29" x 19½")

Norfolk's West Coast

Here we see the reason for the variety of building materials in this corner of Norfolk: layers of limestone, red sandstone and carrstone lie on top of each other, and as the landscape rolls, surface in different places. At Old Hunstanton, the land has been eroded away by the sea in a vertical section, revealing the strata below ground. The limestone bed is also visible on the beach much further east, at West Runton, where it creates lovely rock pools at low tide.

Hunstanton is a lovely place to be on a sunny day; the only place in Norfolk where the afternoon sun glints off the sea, and where it can be watched setting over the sea and the distant Lincolnshire coast.

The Cliffs, Old Hunstanton
2000 (22" x 14½")

Great Snoring
2000 (24" x 9")

One of my favourite roads in Norfolk is the short stretch leading from Fakenham to Wells, via Little Walsingham. The scenery along here is gorgeous, particularly around Houghton St Giles, where the road runs through the valley of the River Stiffkey. On leaving the main A148, the landscape appears rather flat and unpromising initially, until it suddenly dives downhill and sweeps around the spectacular East Barsham Manor, climbing again between tall hedges towards Houghton. Just east of here lie the lovely villages of Great and Little Snoring, Wighton, Warham and Binham. Little Walsingham itself is unusual for Norfolk, having more of the feel of a little town, since most of the buildings abut each other; but then it is an unusual village, being a place of pilgrimage, built around the shrine of Our Lady of Walsingham.

Little Walsingham
1996 (29" x 18½")

Castle Rising

One very bright spring day, I was exploring North-West Norfolk, looking for interesting subject matter, when I drove into Castle Rising. I had not been here for many years, and decided to visit the castle and its grounds. As I walked from the car park towards the imposing earthworks, I was immediately stopped dead in my tracks by the remarkable shadows being cast onto the first mound by a row of pine trees at the perimeter. The scene was perfect, with the castle peeping over the top of the next mound, and the upper branches of a large budding tree glowing red in the sunlight. I took a few photographs of this curiosity, before going to examine the very fine castle. When I returned to the car park after my visit, the shadows had moved round into the ditch, and were quite uninteresting; chance had brought me to the spot at the best possible moment. I later did the painting reproduced here, and still haven't got round to painting the actual castle!

Pine Shadows, Castle Rising
2000 (29" x 12½")

Architectural Masterpieces

Norfolk is greatly blessed with its architectural inheritance, for we have some of the very finest mansions in the country here. Blickling Hall is perhaps my favourite, and was the first property to be taken into care by the National Trust. The roofs and chimneys of these Elizabethan houses are amazing in their extravagance. One pities the poor servants who had to carry the coal and ashes around these vast houses!

There is also much to admire in the smaller-scale buildings of the county; our farmhouses and cottages are remarkably varied, employing an unusually large range of building materials in their walls and roofs. The examples reproduced here are rather limited, as sadly, I do not have photographic records of all the paintings I have produced.

Blickling Hall
2002 (29" x 21")

Felbrigg Hall
2002 (29" x 21")

Norwich Cathedral and the City Skyline from the East
2000 (22" x 14")

Norwich

The paintings I did of Norwich scenes in my student days and just after may have resulted in part from the slightly depressed mood I found myself in at that time. They are not pictures of conventionally beautiful places, although they do represent beauty, in a somewhat quirky way. I was seeking out the beauty to be found in mundane scenes, even though there is a rather bizarre, threatening quality in these paintings of buildings on the point of being demolished. During my time as a student, I had been shocked by the disparate images which the city presented: the glorious showpiece areas such as Elm Hill and the cathedral on the one hand, and some dreadfully neglected parts, such as Magdalen Street, on the other. I was very concerned about this, and made a bit of a nuisance of myself with the planners of the time to try and save a few fine buildings. One thing I discussed with them was the plight of a pair of buildings in Pitt Street, but to no avail; they quickly disappeared, and over thirty years later, the site where they stood is still empty.

Condemned House, Anchor Street
1974, Acrylic on canvas (24" x 36")

Opposite: *Fye Bridge*
1990 (20" x 14")

Since that time, I have stuck to the more conventional beauty spots of the city. It can take quite a long time to work out just how to paint a subject sometimes, and the Norwich pictures have been particularly challenging in this respect. The Norwich Market Place painting, reproduced on the following pages, was a subject I had more or less decided to do in 1994, and I kept going there to look at it, but somehow the light never seemed to look very inspiring, and I just couldn't quite work out why not. I wanted to produce a really stunning, major piece, but I could not make up my mind about the best angle either; whether to take a diagonal view over the top of all the stalls, or perhaps a view from Gentleman's Walk. Most times when I went there, the light was too bland and flat. It wasn't until I found myself overlooking the market early in the year, and at about 12.30, that I realised I had cracked it! At this time of day, provided it is sunny, the sunlight streams along Gentleman's Walk, and catches the façades and signs at a very acute angle, casting fabulous long shadows across all the buildings. The problem of what to do about the incredibly ugly modern building then occupied by Dolcis was also resolved for me on this day. It was very windy, and one or two of the stalls were frying various offerings, so that white smoke and steam was billowing out of some of the stove-pipes above the stalls. This obscured the offending building fairly well, but I also took the liberty of moving a tree slightly to further soften the effect! I decided to depict the Sir Garnet Wolseley pub sign swinging in the wind, as indeed it was, to help illustrate the weather, and I feel that even the flying pigeons help give an illusion of moving air. The picture was painted on an over-size sheet of Arches paper, which is 40" by 30" (or 105cm by 75cm), and turned out to be a major task. After four weeks, I was beginning to want the thing to be finished, and couldn't quite understand why it was taking me so long. In an idle moment, I began to count the window panes I had painted, and this made me realise where the problem lay; after fifteen minutes or so, I had counted 1000 window panes, and there were still a few more left!

The cathedral presented a different kind of problem, which is, that you just cannot find a spot from which you can see the whole structure! This kind of basic fact is one that can be rather easily overlooked; you can make the decision to paint a particular building, but it does pay to look first to discover whether it is actually possible! In the Upper Close, just inside the gates from Tombland, the scene is delightful, with the flowering cherry trees in spring making a perfect calendar picture; but how much of the cathedral can you see? The answer is, not much. I found my favourite angle in the Lower Close, where the other buildings complete the scene beautifully, giving the feeling of the perfect English cathedral close, which of course it is. Five years later, I painted the cathedral from near the river, looking across the Norwich School playing fields (the traditional artist's spot). To try to make my picture a little different, I decided to include as much of the city skyline as possible, in a really panoramic view, taking in City Hall's clock tower, the castle, and the old Shirehall roof (see p.111).

Norwich Cathedral from the Lower Close
1995 (29" x 19")

Overleaf: *Norwich Market Place*
1994 (39½" x 24")

Pull's Ferry
1999 (22" x 14½")

Snow on Mousehold Heath, Norwich
2001 (11½" x 9½")

Farmhouses and Cottages

A Norfolk Farmhouse, near Holt
2001 (29" x 21")

The Old Farmyard
2001 (29" x 19")

East Runton
1995 (29" x 17")

Cottages at Great Walsingham
1998 (21½" x 14")

Field Patterns

I was only twenty years old, and had just started my second year of art school, here in Norwich, when I recall coming to the realisation that landscape painting was what appealed to me most. I can recall the moment quite well; I was walking near my digs at Stoke Holy Cross, and stopped to look at a ploughed field in which the crop was just beginning to break through. It was fairly flat, but still the view over the field and beyond was deeply fascinating; I felt I wanted to try to express the feeling of space that I was experiencing, and the solidity beneath my feet. For me the landscape has a primeval fascination; much of the world is shaped by man's endeavours, and the field patterns in this intensely agricultural area were set out to a great extent centuries ago. I find it very appealing to be able to find a place from which one can view the patchwork-quilt of Norfolk fields, and just daydream.

Field Pattern near Binham
2002 (29" x 16")

Fields at Weybourne
1997 (29" x 19")

Kelling
1997 (29" x 19")

Hedgerow near Cley
1996 (29" x 13")

Two Lanes, Great Walsingham
1996 (29" x 15")

Gamekeeping

Startled Pheasant (Detail from)
2001 (39" x 27")

In late 2000, I accepted a commission from my dentist, to paint a set of views near Frettenham. In his spare time he is an amateur gamekeeper and raises the pheasant chicks in woodland on a large farm there. Thinking that this would be relatively easy, as there is not a building to be seen, I accepted readily. My client then decided on a very large scale for his pictures, and the whole job suddenly grew enormously! I had to study various bird books, and practise painting pheasants until they looked convincing, and the field of sugar-beet reproduced above proved very difficult to paint. However, the finished pictures looked quite imposing.

Maize Cover
2001 (39" x 27")

Tall Oak Wood, Frettenham
2001 (39" x 27")

(Painted as a pair)

Looking West from Cooper's Grove
2001 (39" x 27")

Broadland

Horsey Mere
2000 (11½" x 9")

The Norfolk Broads form a unique and beautiful environment, which has fascinated artists and photographers for centuries. Although I am quite familiar with the area, having done a certain amount of sailing on the Broads, I have to confess to having neglected them a little as a painting subject, as I have been rather distracted by the charms of the coast. I haven't had the use of a boat for the last eleven years either, and there is no doubt that access to the Broads is awkward without a boat. Nevertheless, among others, I have produced the pictures shown here, and I am sure there will be more.

Turf Fen from How Hill
2000 (29" x 19")

Red Sail in the Reeds, Hickling Broad
2000 (10" x 7")

Thatched Boathouse, Hickling Broad
2000 (10" x 7")

Martham Dyke
2000 (11½" x 9")

Woodbastwick
1991 (20" x 15")

Much Further Afield

Terraced Fields, Madeira
2001 (10" x 14")

I've been fortunate to travel to all kinds of places over the years, and here is a selection of some that I have painted. Many of these were painted on the spot, an activity which brings its own challenges, varying from sudden inclement weather, sunburn, attacks by midges in Scotland, to passers-by deciding to tell me about all their relatives who painted. Ann and I went to Madeira on a 'bargain break' early in 2001, and I lugged my painting gear all over the island. I was fascinated by the terraced fields everywhere, and did one or two little pictures of them. To do the painting reproduced here, I climbed over a wall into a bit of wasteland not far from Funchal's Jardim Botanico, and sat leaning against the wall as I worked. A gaggle of delightful young children discovered my hiding place, and came to see what I was up to. They seemed very impressed with my work, and asked me many questions, all in Portuguese. They were not a bit put off by my stock answer of 'Non comprendo', (which actually isn't even Portuguese), and persisted for some time, discovering that patting me on my bald pate was a very effective way of gaining my attention prior to each question! Whereas, I found it just a tad distracting...

Camara de Lobos is a fishing village on Madeira's south coast, and was a favourite place for Sir Winston Churchill to paint; now there is even a restaurant named after him. As I sat painting, I could imagine the great man sitting on the very same spot, with his smock enveloping him, and a large cigar between his lips. Meanwhile, so engrossed was I in my work and my imaginings that I got sunburned!

The Harbour at Camara de Lobos, Madeira
2001 (10" x 14")

Eira do Serrado translates as 'the eagle's eyrie', and is a pass high up in the mountains in the island centre; there are stunning views down into the next valley when one reaches the top, and we walked down a steep winding footpath to the village below. I was stopped in my tracks by this remarkable view over the top of a budding chestnut wood, brightly lit by sunshine, towards a sheer rockface in deep shadow, with a tiny road winding its way around the mountain. This is one of those paintings which almost look like an abstract, until you work out what you are looking at; a concept I like very much.

Mountain Road, Eira do Serrado, Madeira
2001 (22" x 14")

Hovik, Norway
1992 (29" x 10½")

In 1992, I was commissioned by OVDS, one of the three companies operating the Norwegian coastal express steamer service, to produce paintings of their five ships. I did the coastal voyage in late March, and produced quite a number of watercolour sketches from the ship during the trip, many done at breakneck speed while the steamer was travelling. This was the view at one of the many tiny ports on the way, Hovik. It is one of Ann's favourite paintings of mine, perhaps because it looks so peaceful here! They probably don't get too much noise from their neighbours in these parts... One of the ship paintings in question, of the *Finnmarken,* is shown here also, with the vessel in the dramatic far north of Norway in winter.

M.S. Finnmarken *Ofotens og Vesteraalens Dampskibsselskap, Narvik*
1992 (29" x 22")

On this page are a couple of paintings of the Isle of Skye, one seen from the mainland at Mallaig. I made a trip to the Highlands and islands in 1998, in search of a different type of landscape, and returned suitably refreshed and inspired. Ann and I returned to Skye in February of the following year, because I wanted to see snow on the same places I had seen in June. Another reason was to visit the haunts of my favourite band in the world, Runrig, whose music inspires me so much when I am working in the studio.

In the Red Cuillins, Isle of Skye
1999 (29" x 21")

Sunset over the Cuillins, from Mallaig
1999 (29" x 21")

And finally, a couple more paintings of ocean liners. The *Queen Elizabeth 2* will be familiar to most people, and she is seen here arriving in Southampton in 1991.

Queen Elizabeth 2 *Cunard Line*
1991 (20" x 15")

This is more of an historical reconstruction. The *Nieuw Amsterdam* was known as 'the darling of the Dutch'; one of the most beautiful liners ever built, she saw less than one year's service before the outbreak of the Second World War. She was then converted for use as a troopship, a role she served to perfection. After the war, she was refurbished, and this painting shows her around 1947, back in the role she was intended for, departing from New York.

S.S. *Nieuw Amsterdam* *Holland America Line*
2001 (29" x 18")